ENDOR

T0002461

A Drink Called Joy is a brea...

Brother Don brings ... ...
gospel to bear on the issues of our times and offers a
'fresh drink' of God's promise... joy in the power of the
Holy Spirit.

In a woke, permissive, shifting world, where Micah
2:11 could be the mantra of the culture, Brother Don,
shows how the gospel reveals that the word of God and
the presence of Jesus offer the real solution in a world
filled with booze, the smell of legalized marijuana and
compromise all around us.

A few chapter titles tell it best, from *The Taste of
Joy* to *The Dance of Joy*, he brings clarity to an issue
muddled by the culture. Most importantly, he closes
the case powerfully with Isaac, *Hello my name is Laughter* offering practical steps to recapture the joy. This
book will bless you and your family.

—PASTOR BERNIE GILLOTT,
International Evangelism Coordinator,
Global Teen Challenge

A Drink Called Joy is a must read by the body of Christ
and those in faith based recovery. It's simple, insightful,
relevant, and easy to read. Biblical wisdom and application
are found on every single page.

—PASTOR SAINT CLAIR STERLING,
Teen Challenge Jamaica graduate,
and Program Director/Executive Assistant
at Delmarva Adult & Teen Challenge

Pastor Don has done it again! This time he wrote something that I have always felt should have been written. Coming from a lifetime of drinking and drugging, I have always likened my experience with the Holy Ghost with an intoxication of sorts. I believe that the first miracle of Jesus was prophetic to the upper room experience. Both were weddings and both needed wine. You see the wine is what brings the inhibitions down and makes someone brave and willing to fight for what he believes in. Wine makes a man not really care what he looks or sounds like. Wine also has a way of making a man be more loving than he was without it. So I say, "Bring on the wine! Not that old wine that leaves you with regrets, but that New Wine of the Holy Ghost. You know, that *Drink Called Joy*."

—PASTOR JEFF JOHNSON,
Executive Director of Project Hope Texas

I was always chasing joy. But I was baited and tricked by the enemy to embrace a false joy, one that left me more empty and sad than before.

A Drink Called Joy is a fantastic read providing clarity on the addicts need to get "a fix" or "a high" that they're trying to set right within them. They want to get wasted in a sea of goodness, fly above the clouds with a huge smile on their face, freely experiencing all the pleasures they can, but their ignorance or sometimes blatant rebellion leads them to the devils trap... a "counterfeit gladness," as Brother Don calls it.

Whatever God provides us, the enemy provides a counterfeit version. This book helps us see we need to be wise as serpents to discern the difference between getting a worldly high such as heroin, and getting filled with the Spirit. Such peace and happiness await those who leave the world behind and choose eternal joy, riches and ecstasy in Jesus... I'll drink to that!

—MARIAH FREEMAN,
Brother Don's previous secretary, author of
From Heroin to Heaven and joyful mom of five

Bridge-Logos

Newberry, FL 32669

A Drink Called Joy:
A Supernatural Answer To Addiction by Don Wilkerson

Library of Congress Catalog Card Number: 2023935755

International Standard Book Number: 978-1-61036-414-0

Unless otherwise noted, Scripture quotations are from the New King James Version®. Copyright © 1982 by Thomas Nelson. Used by permission. All rights reserved.

Scripture quotations marked (CEV) are from the Contemporary English Version Copyright © 1991, 1992, 1995 by American Bible Society. Used by Permission.

Scripture quotations marked MSG are taken from The Message, copyright © 1993, 2002, 2018 by Eugene H. Peterson. Used by permission of NavPress. All rights reserved. Represented by Tyndale House Publishers.

Scripture quotations marked (NLT) are taken from the Holy Bible, New Living Translation, copyright ©1996, 2004, 2015 by Tyndale House Foundation. Used by permission of Tyndale House Publishers, Carol Stream, Illinois 60188. All rights reserved.

Scripture quotations marked NIV are taken from The Holy Bible, New International Version ®, NIV ®. Copyright © 1973, 1978, 1984, 2011 by Biblica, Inc.® Used by permission. All rights reserved worldwide.

Scripture quotations marked KJV are taken from the King James Version.

Front Cover Design: Todd Wilkerson

Interior Layout and Back Cover Design: Ashley Morgan
GraphicGardenLLC@gmail.com

BP 03/2024

A DRINK CALLED

JOY

A SUPERNATURAL ANSWER TO ADDICTION

DON WILKERSON

BL BRIDGE
LOGOS

Newberry, FL 32669

DEDICATION

To My Wife and Best Friend:
CYNTHIA ANN HUDSON WILKERSON

Thanks for drinking this Joyful Journey with me!
(Special thanks to my son Todd for the
cover design.)

TABLE OF CONTENTS

INTRODUCTION

Sometimes the most obvious things are right in front of our eyes, and we miss them. For me, it was regarding the "supernatural answer to addiction." While working with drug addicts and alcoholics for over 60 years, I often missed the best and clearest remedy for someone to find freedom from addictions of all kinds. What is it?

Joy!

A drink called Joy!

The Apostle Peter refers to the believer's experience of salvation that enables him, or her, to "rejoice with joy unspeakable and full of glory." (1 Peter 1:8) I have heard hundreds of transformed addicts share about this joy they were experiencing. So often, they were at a loss for words in describing their new life that was filled with "joy unspeakable."

I begin this joy ride through the Word and the Spirit by comparing natural joy with supernatural joy. The Bible uses natural things to illustrate and compare with spiritual things: seeds of truth, trees that worship, water representing life, sheep for believers, pasture for where and how the Lord feeds and grazes His sheep. Strangely enough, there are comparisons between unnatural and excessive practices and spiritual practices such as drinking wine in "excess" being condemned; yet this is compared to being "filled with the Spirit." In Ephesians 5:18, Paul writes, "And do not be drunk with wine wherein is excess; but be filled with the Spirit." (KJV)

This is a book in which I use the infilling of the Spirit as the answer and remedy for the use, abuse, and addiction to drugs. I was going to title this, A Drug Called Joy, but felt it would take too much explaining of that title. In the ministry I have been involved in for years, "drink" in that culture is not about drinking water or other beverages. It is about what Paul was indirectly referring to in regard to drinking wine, and not in moderation. But for many, it is part of their lifestyle and they become addicted to it.

I love Paul's contrast between 'spirits' in a bottle or drink and being filled with the Spirit of the living God. The answer to being imbibed with strong drink and drugs of various kinds is to drink in of the Spirit of God.

This is the best answer to drug addiction and alcoholism, and maybe for some, the only answer. As I make my case for *The Supernatural Answer to Addiction*, I will use some of the language of the addict's culture in the manner in which Paul compares those who, in many cases, were wine drinking slaves. They had an unnatural dependency on wine and he in contrast points the believers in Ephesus he wrote to in favor of God dependency on the Lord by drinking in the Holy Spirit of God.

Can I get a witness to that?

Can I get an amen on this?

Maybe instead I should say, "Cheers—I'll drink to that!"

When a group of people sit around a dinner table where wine is served someone may lift a glass, followed by the host saying, "Cheers." Faces will be all smiles. The fellowship is usually good, especially being enhanced by the adult beverage. And there will be one more thing as a result—joy. Natural joy. Of course, it's artificial. It's only temporary, and those having a toast may call it joy, but it's far from the true joy that's known by believers in Christ. When you add the word "super" to "natural," what is the result? An experience in the "Supernatural."

It has been my privilege to witness drug addicts and alcoholics of all types be transformed by God's power, and at the root of it is joy. Revelation 22:17

says, "Come!" say the Spirit and the Bride. Whoever hears, echo, "Come!" Is anyone thirsty? Come! All who drink, come and drink, drink freely of the Water of Life!" (MSG) Those that drink this drink find satisfaction that nothing else can compare. This joy when possessed is like the fountainhead of "Rivers of living water [that] will brim and spill out of the depths of anyone who believes in me this way." (John 7:38 MSG)

I consider myself to be a Spirit-filled Christian, a Spirit-filled preacher, teacher, and writer. I come from the Assemblies of God denomination that is (or at least, used to be) a strong proponent of receiving the Baptism of the Holy Spirit. One of the evidences of the infilling of the Spirit being speaking in "other tongues" as happened in the Upper Room in the book of Acts.

Note that the doctrine (if it can be called that) of the infilling of the Holy Spirit as evidenced by speaking in an unknown tongue is taught by Pentecostals traditionally as "the initial physical evidence" of the Baptism of the Holy Spirit. It is not the only evidence. Since it is the experience of the "Holy Spirit," it's about two things: "Holy" and "Spirit," and both are essential. In other words, the other important evidence is living a holy lifestyle.

I am not advocating for all believers to speak in other tongues, but for myself, I can say as with the Apostle Paul, "I thank my God I speak with tongues more than you all." (I Corinthians 14:18)

One evidence of a Spirit-filled person that I missed when teaching about the Person and work of the Holy Spirit, one I seemed to have missed that is so obvious is that of joy. In my research for this book, I noticed that there are very few books on the subject of joy. C.S. Lewis' book, *Surprised by Joy,* is one. I was, and am, surprised more attention has not been given to joy in a believer's life. It is the second fruit of the Spirit, listed right after love.

If you are currently an addict, then find a place that serves *A Drink Called Joy.* If you are in recovery, then let joy be your strength. (Nehemiah 8:10) Cultivate joy by being in a Sprit-filled atmosphere. If you have a loved one in bondage to some type of life-controlling problem, seek out a place where your loved one can find *A Drink Called Joy.* It is *The Supernatural Answer to Addiction.*

C.S. Lewis writes in *The Case for Christianity*, "If a thing is free to be good it is also free to be bad. A free will is what made evil possible. Why, then, did God give them free will? Because freewill, though it makes Evil possible, also makes possible any love or goodness or joy worth having."[1]

I recognize that many Christians do drinking wine in moderation, and it is part of the culture in many countries. So it was in Paul's day. Both then and today drinking in excess is both physically and spiritually unhealthy. For those who when it comes to the "moderate" or the "excessive" I recommend a better brand of drink—a heavenly one provided by the indwelling of the Spirit. We drink some-thing every day. Let it also and always include *A Drink Called Joy*. "Relying on God has to begin all over again every day as if nothing had yet been done." (C.S. Lewis)[2]

Chapter 1

THE MOST "HIGH" GOD

"I will be glad and rejoice in You;
I will sing praise to Your name, O Most High."

Psalm 9:2

"No soul that seriously and constantly desires
joy will ever miss it. Those who seek find.
To those that knock it is opened."

—C.S. Lewis[3]

I would add to the above Lewis quote: Those that drink in joy will keep drinking and drinking until it becomes the central thing in their life. A new "high" for some.

As I write this, the Jesus Revolution documentary is playing in theaters. It is about the Jesus Movement in the late 1960's and early 70's. When Pastor Chuck Smith asked a former hippie-drug

1

user why so many of his generation were coming to Jesus to be saved, he responded, "They're looking for a new high."

In the ministry of Teen Challenge that my brother and I founded, we had already heard and seen that even hardcore addicts were looking for that very same high. In the early 70's, during the hippie movement, people were using and "getting high" on a multiplicity of drugs; not just marijuana or heroin.

My friend and co-worker Mike Zello, Sr. founded Teen Challenge in the Washington, D.C. area. Mike worked for my brother David even before I did. He shared the following with me:

"Mind altering and mood changing drugs were commonly used, as well. As a result, some were admitted into psychiatric facilities. One such place was in Crownsville, Maryland. We accepted patients from there into our Washington, D.C. Adult and Teen Challenge Christian faith-based residential discipleship program.

One guy that arrived told me that he wound up in Crownsville because he was tripping on LSD and had a bad trip. He thought he was invincible and could drive through the stack of cars in front of him that were waiting for the red light to change. So, he floored the gas pedal and plowed into the cars. While with us, God delivered him from his addiction, healed his mind, saved him and filled him with the Holy Spirit.

He said, "I got high on a lot of different kinds of drugs, but I have never been this high before." He began to read and enthusiastically study the Bible. One of the verses he read was Psalm 57:2: "I will cry to God Most High, to God who accomplishes all things for me."

He said, "There it is! Now I know why I feel so good. With all the drugs I did, I never felt this high before." He concluded that the reason why he felt so high was because he allowed God into his life. He said, "God is the Most High God and you can't get any higher than that!"

The amazing thing about God is that He can speak to us in the language and terminology we understand. In this respect, I use two words that seem totally opposite each other: the word "drink" and the word "joy," these two words together. I propose to show that joy is like what a drunk or drug addict experiences on a high; that once true joy from the Most High God is tasted and experienced, that joy will win out every time. Discovering this came as a revelation to me.

When I first began working with drug addicts (almost all heroin users) when they encounter Jesus Christ some of them would talk about being "high" on God or "high" on the Holy Spirit. I never rebuked them about this, but I thought it was not a way to describe what a person experiences through knowing the Lord. But I've learned that God can communicate with us in the language, culture, and even subculture we are familiar with.

As I write this, there is an advertisement on television called, "He Gets Us" about how Christ wants to be relevant to all people. God understands and gets what we need. He gets the rich, the poor, the Wall Street Executive and the homeless drug addict referred to above. And certainly He gets the drug abuser, alcoholic, and addicts in general. One thing that they need in contrast to what a drug or drink gives them—they need the joy of the Lord.

The idea for my comparing a drink at a bar with the Christian's joy came from Apostle Paul's writing in Ephesians 5:18: "And be not drunk with wine, wherein is excess; but be filled with the Spirit." (KJV) I asked myself, "Why does Paul make a contrast between spirits in a bottle and the Holy Spirit? Does this mean that there are similarities on how the Spirit affects us and how alcohol and or drugs affect us? To me, there is no other valid reason for such a comparison. Also, perhaps Paul was thinking what happened on the day of Pentecost when Peter said of those who experienced a rushing mighty wind and tongues of fire. He responded, "These are not drunk, as you suppose." (Acts 2:15) This means they appeared to be drunk in the only way known at that time.

Putting this in some contemporary language, we might also say, "Don't try to get all your satisfaction out of a shopping spree (or some other activity), but instead be filled with the One who can satisfy your deepest longings."

In Dr. H.A. Ironside's commentary he wrote: "You will notice he [Paul writing in Eph. 5:18] puts two things in opposition, the one to the other —drunkenness with wine and the filling of the Holy Spirit. Why does he contrast these two things, these two conditions? You see, the man with over-imbibing, the man who is drunk with wine, is controlled by a spirit foreign to himself. Men, when they are under the control of the spirit of alcohol, do and say things they would never do in their normal condition. They make fools of themselves, they descend to all kinds of ribaldry and nonsense, and people say, excusing them, "Oh, well; you mustn't hold it against him. He was drunk. He was not himself."

"Apostle Paul says that condition should never be true of a Christian, but on the other hand the Christian should be dominated and controlled by the Holy Spirit of God, and in the power of the Holy Spirit of God... and be enabled to say and do what he could not say and do in his merely natural condition."[4]

So the answer as to why Paul compares drunkenness by the spirits in a bottle to the Holy Spirit is control. We are either controlled by sin in all its manifestations or controlled by the Holy "Spirit." One causes out-of-control behavior and the other produces sanity, serenity, love, peace, and joy.

Joy is the best alternative and answer to being addicted to a drug and or alcohol. It can be a "high" without adverse after effects. Joy puts you into a state of mind that is one of peace. I do not know why it's taken me so long to realize that joy in Jesus and in the Spirit is so far greater than any drug or alcohol experience. Furthermore, the Holy Spirit's "hangover" will never give you a headache, a regret, a criminal record, or a loss of self-respect including from family members, spouses, and society in general. If you have not done so yet, give up your narcotic drug connection and connect with Jesus through the Holy Spirit. As the man talked about above, you connect with the Most "High" God. Let your prayer be as David writes in Psalm 57:2, "I will cry to God the Most High, to God who performs all things for me."

Drugs trick the brain into thinking it is the answer to all the user's insecurities, emptiness in life, hurts, fears, and broken relationships.

Joy is a fruit of the Spirit listed in Galatians 5:22, right after "love." The reason I believe that the best and only cure for addiction is found in the words of a hymn that has a line in it from 1 Peter 1:8 saying that those that believe in Jesus Christ can "rejoice with joy unspeakable and full of glory." C.S. Lewis wrote: "Joy is the serious business of heaven."[5]

I do believe that not only is joy a fruit of the Spirit, but it is also an evidence of being filled with the Holy Spirit. However, I also believe that the salvation experience in and of itself alone can be for some a joyful high. My wife grew up in a Methodist church, but never was "born again" as that was never taught in her church. In her senior year of high school a group from an evangelical Christian school—Houghton College—made a presentation in a Sunday service. Cynthia Hudson responded and accepted Christ that day. She says of that experience, "I remember I had such joy."

Isaiah 12:3 says, "Therefore with joy you will draw water from the well of salvation." If any person calls themselves a disciple of Jesus and does not have joy, they should question whether they are saved or not.

This leads me to the subject of this book. Joy trumps a drug or alcohol high. If any drug addict or alcoholic can tell me that living a life in Christ in which He puts within a believer a river of living water "springing up into everlasting life" (John 4:14) is not better than what he had before, I'd like to hear about it.

After my wife was saved, she went to a high school dance. She was dancing with a classmate who was a friend (but not a boyfriend) and she said to him, "Guess what? Sunday in church I accepted Christ into my heart."

He responded, "Then what are you doing here?" She had never given a thought that she was doing wrong because going to that dance she felt was the best place to tell someone else about her joy. C.S. Lewis wrote: "I sometimes wonder whether all pleasures are not substitutes for joy."[6] Lewis was on to something—*A Drink Called Joy.*

Chapter 2

POWER, POWER, WONDER-WORKING POWER

*"This is what the L*ORD *says:*
'Stop at the crossroads and look around, ask for the
old, godly way, and walk in it. Travel its path, and
you will find rest for your souls.'" But you reply,
"No, that's not the road we want."

Jeremiah 6:16 NLT

"He who seeks not the cross of Christ
seeks not the glory of Christ." [7]

—John of the Cross

I am sharing about the supernatural remedy to addiction, using stories from the years of ministering to addicts. They, the transformed ones, have found a new and changed life by experiencing the joys of salvation and deliverance. I will share yet another one here from the early days of the founding of Teen Challenge. But I must pause before telling this next story.

There are those that try to tell me that it's a new day working with addicts and we must reach them in new ways. One person told me, "Don, these are not the 1970's anymore in Teen Challenge." In the course of a 15-to-20-minute conversation, he mentioned at least three times that "These are not the 70's anymore." I think he was trying to say that our program and fund-raising polices need to change. I'm not sure if he was condoning the medical model in place of the faith-based, Christ-centered program. I call the latter "The Gospel on Day One" approach to addiction. They cannot do this, if receiving non-faith based, public taxpayer funds! This person may have not been advocating this, but others in the ministry I have been co-founder of are doing just that. If he was, I feel sorry for him. How anyone can say the gospel is outdated, I cannot understand. I am passionate about the responsibility of a mission true, Christ-centered, faith-based rehab program, sharing the saving gospel of Jesus from Day One.

Now I will tell my story that took place in the late 1960's. During our chapel services, we sang out of hymnbooks that had been donated to us. In each meeting I led, I would pick out hymns for the worship part of the service. Who sings out of hymnbooks today? I suppose some do, but I have not in decades. We had no curriculum then as we do now for students. Singing the hymns was the closest thing we had for providing biblical teaching, as that was the original purpose of hymn singing.

During some of those daily chapel services when the students had sung certain hymns more than once, I'd ask, "What hymn would you want us to sing now?' Almost invariably, it was the one entitled, "There's Power in the Blood." We sang it so often that I began to call it "The National Anthem of Teen Challenge."

It took some years to ask myself why—that among so many great hymns these drug addicts learned—why this particular one, There's Power In The Blood, was so meaningful to them?

Then it came to me. A line in it says, "Would you be free from the burden of sin? There's power, wonder-working power in the blood of the Lamb." These were hardcore heroin addicts who knew all about the power of drugs in their blood stream, a power that captivated them. In their own terminology, they described it as having "a monkey on their back" who would not let go. They knew both the pleasure and destructive power of drugs. They knew what they had to do every day to get money to feed the monkey: rob, steal, con, connive and do things they never would have believed they would wind up doing.

But now they had come to a place where they were finding hope and help by hearing the Gospel from Day One. In this hymn about the Power in the Blood, they heard about a greater power, a saving, healing power that could enable them to be set free, and free forever. As I would preach to them about The Old Rugged Cross and they would sing the 'Power in the Blood" hymn, I would say, "God will give you power to have power over power." That power was explained how sin is forgiven, and the same power that raised Christ from the dead could dwell in them, if they asked. (Romans 6:4-5)

There was a desire in most of them to have this other kind of power helping them to overcome the power that heroin had over them. Those who wanted that power could ask for it, find it, enjoy it and find that Drink called Joy. Joy is at the root and origin of salvation's transformation that begins with the blood of Jesus shed on the cross. That blood was spilt for the forgiveness of sin and to reconcile us to God through Christ's suffering on the cross. Joy, therefore, is only possible because "God was in Christ, reconciling the world to Himself" (2 Corinthians 5:19), enabling all who call on Him to be given a fresh start by offering forgiveness of sins. This experience results in, among other things, joy. I never get tired of seeing and witnessing such captives set free and having this Drink called Joy.

I say to those who think we need to reach more addicts, who would argue against that? I agree. But if the so-called reaching means compromising the gospel, then those who want to increase the number of reached without "old things passing away and all things becoming new" through Jesus Christ (2 Corinthians 5:17), I will continue to speak out against this. You can have your numbers; I'll take gospel results instead of numbers without transformations. I watched as a leader of what used to be an authentic mission boast about "reaching" thousands or more addicts and there was no mention of saving their souls.

Even King David got in trouble with God over numbers. (Read 2 Samuel 24) I say to you if you're now still in your addiction: do you want to be listed as someone's "number" with your name written down in their books as they profit financially from your addiction—or do you want your name written down in "The Lamb's book of Life"? (Revelation 20:15; 22:19) I recognize that with an epidemic of opioid addiction and other drugs of choice resulting in addiction, that they need a place for detox and some form of treatment. But treatment has become a business, enriching those who offer it. Ministry is and should be different. Why copy the secular forms of treatment?

Tozer wrote, "Never do the disciples use gimmicks to attract crowds. They count on the power of the Spirit to see them through all the way. They gear their activities to Christ and are content to win or lose along with Him. The notion that they could set up a "programmed" affair and use Jesus as a kind of a sponsor never so much as entered their heads. To them, Jesus was everything."[8]

He "still is" to the majority of my colleagues.

During my early days in the 70's, a woman interviewed me at Brooklyn Teen Challenge. She was doing a paper on the different modalities of drug treatment. I gave her a description of who we were and how we worked with addicts. She then asked to interview a student. I suspected in asking this she had an agenda. So I picked out a student with a lot of street smarts as well as gospel smarts. After the young lady got this young man's drug history, he also shared about all the other programs he'd been unsuccessful in. She asked, "What's different about this place? What are you getting here you did not get elsewhere?"

His answer is a classic. He said, "Well ma'am— they give us God the Father in the morning, Jesus in the afternoon, and the Holy Spirit in the evening."

She responded, "It sounds like you're using God as a crutch."

"You're right! I got two of them. Oh sorry, three crutches."

Someone said to me this sounds too "simplistic." The gospel is not that hard to figure out. Jesus does for the addict what he or she cannot do for themselves. He brings the enslaved sinner into His courtroom, pronounces us guilty, then forgives our trespasses and we're free to go and enjoy our new life. This is the "joy unspeakable" Peter writes about in First Peter 1:8.

The same woman mentioned above asked a question I've been asked not infrequently: "How many make it who graduate from Teen Challenge?"

My answer is simply: "Anyone who wants to! Jesus said, 'The one who comes to Me I will by no means cast out.'" (John 6:37)

(I recommend watching a 28-minute documentary entitled, *The Remedy: No Other Cure.* Available on YouTube. A Brooklyn Teen Challenge Production)

Chapter 3

THE TASTE OF JOY

*"Oh, taste and see that the LORD is good;
Blessed is the man that trusts in Him."*

Psalm 34:8

*"I know of no greater need today
than the need for joy. Unexplainable,
contagious joy. Outrageous joy."*

—Charles Swindoll[9]

It goes without saying that drugs can both kill and save lives, destroy or heal. That is true when the drug is used in a right manner. Millions have a better quality of life because of useful drugs. It is the abuse of drugs and alcohol that leads to fatal addictions that turn a once respectable person into a garbage container for all sorts of narcotics and various forms of adult beverages. During covid, a drug may have saved my life.

On April 1st in 2020, I was in an emergency vehicle being transferred from my home to a hospital in Culpepper, Virginia. It was my second such trip within a few days. The first was when I was incapable of walking, dehydrated, had very serious diarrhea, and was unable to eat or smell. Both my wife and I tarts did not think I had covid, but eventually all the signs pointed to that. It was confirmed in the emergency unit at the hospital, but not for four days later because the turnaround time then for testing covid took that long,

I got the call confirming it from a woman at the Virginia Department of Health. She confirmed that yes, I had tested positive for covid plus I had a touch of pneumonia. I then realized how serious my case was. She suggested I go immediately back to the hospital. So, as I rode in the EMS vehicle I asked the attendant what day it was. He said Sunday, April 1st. I laughed and said, "How fitting! April Fool's Day." Later I concluded that a few weeks prior I made the foolish mistake of taking an Amtrak train to New York City when warnings were already out about how the virus spread. I was a victim of that epidemic which was in its early stages.

The hospital, I think, gave me antibiotic medicine. I had a sleepless first night. In the morning a doctor came to see me and asked if I wanted to take the hydroxychloroquine drug (at the time the pharma industry had not yet succeeded in getting it banned).I said yes, not thinking much about it one way or the other.

The next morning, I saw my breakfast tray by my bedside. I had not touched the last four meals they had brought me because of my loss of appetite and smell. But this time I saw a cup of orange juice and took a sip. I think I drank the whole cup. I then called Cindy, my wife, all excited.

I said to her, "Honey, I can taste! I can taste! I can taste!"

Yes, three times I said it. It was pure joy!

The next day the doctor said all my vital signs were good and that I might as well go home. I took the drug for five more days plus the antibiotics. Within a week to ten days, I was back to normal. Cindy also had the virus, but it didn't impact her in the way it did me. In my case, I attributed the fact I had an Asian doctor who knew what medicine I needed as an answer to prayer of people who knew I had covid and were praying for me.

Now, I'd rather have not wanted to experience the covid effects that I did and the remarkable way

I recovered to experience that joy I felt in the hospital from just some orange juice. But I will never forget the feeling I had when my taste and smell and appetite came back to me.

Joy tasted so good.

I have always loved and quoted often in sermons I preached Psalm 34:7, "Oh taste and see that the LORD is good." As covid began to take many lives, my joy became even greater that the Lord used what would become a banned drug to potentially save my life (although when experiencing covid, the thought of dying never entered my mind).

Why do the Scriptures use the word taste in respect to the goodness of the Lord? Because in the natural we can relate to the word. To taste something—liquid, solid food—is to experience something enjoyable (especially if you're Italian). Since taste in the natural is an enjoyment, how much more in the spiritual and in the supernatural. My purpose in sharing this, besides being a testimony to the answered prayers for me and Cindy from people from around the world, is to write about the importance of joy in our lives.

It is time for joy. Even a revival of joy! It's one thing to have a personal experience of joy such as my wife and I did during covid, but it's another thing to talk about joy on a larger scale.

Nevertheless, any movement is only effective if it is happening at the grassroots of our lives. What could a taste of joy look like if spread like a virus on the scale of covid? Might the best medicine for us be "a merry heart"? (Proverbs 17:22)

I can hear it as far away from California to my home in Virginia: "Is it really a time for joy?" The world's a mess. The threat of nuclear war hangs over us. National and internationally conditions are the worst in decades. From the gas pump to the grocery store, we're paying the price of whoever is supposed to be in charge of regulating these things.

Is it really a time for joy? Yes! Yes! What better time for the sunshine of joy to burst through the dark clouds that hang over us. It is time for a revival of joy in our hearts and homes and especially the church. Present day prophets may differ as to whether there will be a last day's revival. I'm on the side of the revivalists. The revival I look for would be one in which believers will have an overdose of joy!

On a small scale, this revival of joy has been happening in faith-based rehab programs like Teen Challenge and those patterned after it. Many former drug addicts and alcoholics amending salvation in Jesus Christ. The infilling of the Holy Spirit of joy is just the antidote and cure they need to be set free from the slavery of a life-controlling problem.

Do you have that joy? If so, share it. If not, then "Taste and see that the Lord is good." All of life is better when Christ dwells within you. Everything tastes better when we know the Lord. What do you do when your whole life is depending on a powder, pill, or liquid fix to satisfy you? What do you do when you stop? What do you replace it with? Pardon the pun, but why not try the gos-pill.

C.S. Lewis writes in The Case for Christianity the following (I quoted this before, but it bears repeating). "If a thing is free to be good, it is also free to be bad. And free will is what made evil possible. Why, then, did God give them free will? Because freewill, though it makes evil possible, also makes possible any love or goodness or joy worth having."[10]

I wrote in my Challenge Study Bible a commentary on Psalm 30:11-12 in which David wrote: "You have turned my sorrow into joyful dancing. No longer am I sad wearing sackcloth, I will never stop singing Your praises, my Lord and my God." I wrote on these verses, "Think of a time when you could have gone down in a pit. Maybe you've been saved from a life-threatening illness, an accident that could have happened, but didn't, a substance abuse that could have been fatal. David had a night of wailing; things miraculously changed for the better. Has any of this happened to you? Then let your heart sing for joy and give God the praise."

In a time of an epidemic of opioid addiction destroying lives living and dead, may joy be spread as a revolutionary, supernatural treatment for addiction. It is a gift God waits to give. Joy is one of the many benefits of salvation in Jesus Christ—and one of the best. Oh, taste and see!

I will drink to that! Will you?

Chapter 4

"JOHN SMOKED ME"

*"On your feet now—applaud God! Bring a gift of
laughter, sing yourselves into his presence."*
Psalm 100:1 The Message

*"The most wasted of all days is one
without laughter."*
—E.E. Cummings[11]

Joy and laughter go together. Karl Barth said,
"Laughter is the closest thing to the grace of
God."[12] In my preaching and writing, I insert
humor, but not jokes. I find humor in natural
things and supernatural things. To write about joy,
I must include a story I've told many times which
has gone around the world. At the end of the story,
most people have a good, sanctified laugh. The
story comes from Johannesburg, South Africa

brought back by my co-worker at the time, Mike Zello, Sr. (Also the story in Chapter One about The Most "High" God came from Mike as well). First, a little background on this story.

Years ago, I was with my brother David when he spoke at an outdoor venue in Johannesburg. A young African came back with us to America to train and then return to his homeland to reach troubled youth. He opened an evangelistic outreach coffeehouse similar to one my mother operated at the time in Greenwich Village called "The Lost Coin."

Over the years, that ministry in South Africa saw many souls come to Christ and 13 of them ended up in the ministry. One of them became the pastor of a mega church in Johannesburg. I hope one of the other 12 became the street preacher in the story that follows. I have no proof of it and I have no way of telling. But what is shared in this story is true to life.

Once a week a young street preacher in Johannesburg went to a park where hippies, drug users, and the homeless hung out. He stood on a bench and preached. Afterwards he invited any listeners to receive Christ. One such fellow did not accept Jesus, but nevertheless he approached the preacher and asked him for his Bible. He said, "Preacher, may I have your Bible?"

It was a New Testament. The preacher asked, "Why do you want this?"

He answered, "I'll be honest with you, I see how thin the paper is it's printed on. Those pages would be very good to roll a marijuana smoke."

The preacher looked long and hard at him, and had an inspiration. "I'll tell you what! I will give this Bible/New Testament to you, but on one condition. You read the page before you smoke it."

"I promise you I will do that," the longhaired hippie type responded.

Fast forward two years later. The preacher finishes his outdoor message and a young man walks up to him. He was dressed in a suit. Clean shaved. Shiny shoes. He says, "Preacher, do you remember me?"

"No! Can't say that I do? Should I know you?"

"Well, I was here in this very park and listened to you preach. Then I asked for your Bible that I found out was a New Testament," the handsome man explained.

The preacher says, "Oh yes! Now I remember. I asked you to read a page before you smoked it. What happened to you?"

"I did what you asked...

I smoked Matthew!

I smoked Mark!

I smoked Luke!

Then John smoked me!"

Now if you did not get a joyful laugh out of that, you need to get saved. Why do I share this story and testimony? I know it will always get a laugh and to me laughter is an expression of joy. I don't think laughter needs to be sensual, hateful, political or meaningless. For those who love God and drink at the Fountain of Living Water, it can be spiritual as well. I include this story also because I know the joy—and miracles—that happen when the gospel is shared in open-air outreaches. My wife and I began our ministry on the streets of Brooklyn. I shared about this in a book my wife and I recently wrote entitled, *The Girl in the Red Dress.* In it we have a chapter called, "Taking Jesus to the Streets" (This book is available on Amazon). Today the streets have been taken over by protesters, criminals, the homeless and addicts and it's time for joy-pushers to "Go into the highways and hedges, and compel them to come in, so My house may be filled." (Luke 14:23) Wherever this is done (in Johannesburg or Brooklyn), when we reach out to the lost, we are doing God's work.

Speaking of my wife, my wife makes me laugh! To me, her spirituality is at times her expression of joy. If a British movie is on TV, she can mimic their British accents perfectly. Once, while watching the movie, *Out of Africa,* she sounded exactly like the female star. She made me laugh so hard, and that to me was better than the movie.

When I drive too slowly, she calls me an old man. If I drive too fast, she does not say a word. She just hits her left thigh a number of times and I get the message. If I wait too long at a traffic light when it changes from red to green, she says, "It's not going to get any greener!"

After shopping recently for groceries, I picked her up. Whence got in the car, she told me, "I was in a long line to pay for my groceries when a man in the next aisle motioned me to come to his register. She said, "Boy was he ever checking me out!" She smiled over sharing the double meaning of being "checked out. "Yes, my wife makes me laugh and brings joy into our marriage.

We often do not realize that joy with laughter is a part of spirituality. If you are in recovery and experienced salvation and *A Drink Called Joy*, you may have never realized that being in Christ is not boring. It is meant to be one of the most joyous things you will ever experience in life.

If you're having a bad day, find someone who makes you laugh and your bad day may not turn out so bad. If you have or find such a person, you have found someone spiritual; maybe even Spirit-filled. I bet you never equated spirituality with laugher, and laughter with joy, and joy as evidence of a Spirit-filled life. One of my closest friends in life is Jesse Owens (not the runner). He is one of the most upbeat persons I've ever known. He is full of joy and a joy pusher. No one can ever be gloomy for long around him.

If you serve a leader, have a spouse, or know someone who's too uptight, tell them to "lighten up," and read my book!

At my brother David's funeral, I shared a funny story about me and him. It was what I thought in good taste. Yet, one of my brother's Board members rebuked me for it. I still am shaking my head over that. Everyone in the audience laughed at what I said.

I was not invited to go back to a certain church where I spoke occasionally because the pastor's wife did not like me mixing humor with theology. One person commented on my preaching saying, "Pastor, I love how you use humor to disarm people. Then, bam, you hit them with an important truth by the Sword of the Lord."

When I end the above story from Johannesburg, there of course is laughter—and once I almost regretted telling it as I thought I had lost the congregation. Maybe it was because I ended the story by saying, "Holy smokes!" LOL!

Chapter 5

HAPPY HOUR

"You have given me greater joy than those who have abundant harvests of grain and new wine."

Psalm 4:7 NLT

"Joy is peace dancing; peace is joy resting."
—Author unknown

As previously stated, drug addicts and alcoholics, when seeking after a supernatural cure, often view spiritual things through the prism of their past or present addiction. This was true when a resident of a faith-based discipleship rehab called his brothers to chapel announcing it was "Happy Hour." I picked up on that and said that in a bar that serves drinks "Happy Hour" may be from 5 P.M. to 7 P.M., but when you serve the Lord it's 24/7.

Paul's contrast between indulging in excessive drink/wine in comparison to the infilling of the Spirit is not the only such reference in the Bible. Psalm 4:7 says, "You have put gladness in my heart more than in the season that their grain and wine increase." I recall after preaching in our faith-based rehab chapel, during an altar time, there was usually another extended time and season of praise and worship. Everyone who was at the altar returned to their seats and were standing. At such times, I often don't know how to end the service. Pastors know the same. Or, at least I hope they do. When this happens in a chapel full of addicts having found the Lord, or are on the verge of doing so, it is usually a time when the seekers outnumber the non-seekers. It makes the work of rehab-discipleship much easier.

When I see or hear students wanting more time to worship, more time to enjoy A DRUG CALLED JOY in the Holy Spirit's Happy Hour, I'm reminded of Psalm 4:7 quoted above and as written in The Message. It reads like this:

> *Why is everyone hungry for more? "More, more,"*
> *they say.*
> *"More, more."*
> *I have God's more-than-enough,*
> *More joy in one ordinary day*
> *Than they get in all their shopping sprees.*
> (Psalm 4:7 MSG)

If any place and persons need a Holy Spirit Happy Hour, it's those who are seeking to come out of a lifestyle of counterfeit gladness. I heard a sermon years ago entitled, A Drink at Joel's Bar based on Joel 2:28 that says, "I will pour out My Spirit on all flesh." In many faith-based Christ-centered rehab ministries, this happens on a regular basis.

I have 60 plus years of experience working with addicts and I'm an eyewitness to faith-based programs that present a supernatural cure to addiction through Jesus Christ and by the power of the Holy Spirit. However, such programs can be like any church where the presence of the Holy Spirit may or may not be visibly present. There are churches that are dry and others that are alive in the Spirit. There are churches that can be evangelical, but not evangelistic; they can be formal, yet never preach and see people encounter Christ— so it is with some faith-based programs. If you are in a program that calls itself faith-based, but in truth, it is fake-based (trading off a faith-based name for their organization, but in reality more secular than spiritual) and if you can leave, then do so. But if you are mandated to be there or are settled into the program, it may be best for you to tough it out.

When I write as a subtitle to this book about A Supernatural Answer to Addiction, I'm referring to a supernatural experience made available to those coming out of addiction. There is a difference between God's Presence and a Program—especially if it is not faith-based.

I hope no one is offended by my interpretation of Jesus' first miracle at the wedding at Cana. In light of the subject of this book, I see that miracle as a contrast between an unhappy hour and a Happy Hour. Mary said to Jesus, "They have no wine." (John 2:3) A church or rehab ministry that quenches the Holy Spirit does not have the wine of the Spirit. My wife and I once sat in such a chapel service, and all I could think is what Mary said to Jesus: "They have no wine."

I asked an intern at a very large rehab program, one that used to graduate over 200 students a year, "How would you rate the Chapel services at your place now on a scale of 1 to 10?" He laughed and said, "It's a cookie cutter service. One chapel is the same as another." In other words, "They have no wine." No wonder they graduate now less than 10% of the number of graduates when they once served up *A Drink Called Joy*.

Jesus turned water into what I believe was sweet wine, not fermented, and the master host of the wedding said, "You have kept the good wine until now." (John 2:10) Thus, this miracle was about celebration—about joy.

Three things happen when there is a Holy Spirit inspired "Happy Hour" in a church or ministry program.

1. **There is vibrant worship led by a Spirit-filled worship leader and or a worship team.**

   The verse I have based this book on is Ephesians 5:18 where excessive drinking of wine is compared to being filled with the Holy Spirit. The next verse describes what a Spirit-filled Happy Hour should consist of: "Speaking to one another in psalms and hymns and spiritual songs, singing and making melody in your heart to the Lord." (Ephesians 5:19)

   "Eternal joy is not reached by living on the surface. It is rather attained by breaking through the surface, by penetrating the deep things of ourselves, our world, and our God. The moment in which we reach the last depth of our lives is the moment in which we can experience joy that has eternity within it, the hope that cannot be destroyed, and the truth of which life and death is built. For in the depth of that truth; and in the depth is hope; and in the depth is joy." (Paul Tillich)[13]

2. **When there is serious prayer at times of scheduled prayer in the church and ministries, as well as when worshipper-seekers gather around the**

altar following the preaching and teaching of God's Word, this too is a Happy Hour.

The physical gathering around an altar is an outward expression of a believer's inward desires. We of course can pray and worship the Lord whether in the last or first row of the church. But the simple act of leaving one's place to go forward to seek the Lord indicates holy desire. Jonathan Edwards preached in a sermon that "The heartfelt praise of one true believer is more precious to God than all the 220,000 oxen and the 120,000 sheep Solomon offered to God at the dedication of the temple."[14]

3. **The result of serious prayer and worship is that the presence of the Lord and joy will be the evident.**

Elisha said, "Send someone who can play the harp." (2 Kings 3:15) An unusual alliance was formed between the tribes of Israel and the King of Edom (normally an enemy of Israel) to go to war against King Mesha of Moab. As they marched through the desert, the water supply ran out, so they sought a prophet to inquire of God. They found Elisha [instead], who said, "Go talk to the prophets of the foreign gods your parents worshipped. They said, "No, they had to inquire of God." Elisha replied, "I serve the Lord All-Powerful." He said he would ask the Lord

All-Powerful, but bring me someone who can play the harp (v. 15). As the harp played, the word of the Lord came to Elisha and he prophesied, saying they would defeat Moab's army. The next morning the water flowed so much there was a flood—and they were in the desert! Note that the miracle happened during morning devotions (v. 20). Thank God for gifted musicians, worship leaders, singers and songwriters who help us express our praise and worship" [and that brings joy]. (From The Challenge Study Bible)

Elisha calling for the harp was a call to worship. Joy is God's Secret Weapon for Every Believer. (The title of a book by Georgian Banov).

● Chapter 6 ●

"MORE, MORE, MORE!"

"I will hope continually, and will yet praise you more and more. My mouth will tell of your righteousness and your salvation all day long, for I do not know their limits."

Psalm 71:14-15

"The most valuable thing the Psalms do for me is express the same delight in God which made David dance."

—C.S. Lewis[15]

One of my favorite places to preach is a Teen Challenge chapel service. I have done so in Centers all over the world. One Friday night at Brooklyn Teen Challenge as I was finishing speaking, my usual custom was to have students invited around the altar for prayer. Myself and coworkers prayed for the women and men who were seeking after God. As the music and worship continued, eventually everyone returned to their seats. Most remained standing and the praise and worship continued. When our worship leaders, Mary and Will Kitchen, tried to conclude the service, some of the students hollered out, "More, more, more!" They didn't want the meeting to stop. They wanted to worship more. I was sitting in the back at that point. Needless to say, I was moved by what I saw and heard.

In another chapel service just like that one, one of the things that I would preach to the students is this: "We are not here to help you get your life back. If you get it back, you'll probably just mess it up again. We're here to help you give your life away. To give it to God. To seek after God."

I realize not all chapel or church services are going to be an occasion for asking for more; but there needs to be more of them. I share with leaders of recovery programs, "In your chapel, there may be a thermometer that tells you the climate in the place. There is however, another kind of climate you should know; that is, what is the spiritual thermostat of your ministry? As a leader, it is your responsibility to gauge it, and if it's cold or lukewarm, pray down the fire of God."

Paul, in writing about being filled with the Spirit (Ephesians 5:18) wrote the following: "Speaking to one another in psalms, hymns and spiritual songs, singing and making melody in your hearts to the Lord." When that happens, it's like "a drink at Joel's Bar." That was the title of a message I read based on Joel 2:28, "And it shall come to pass afterward that I will pour out my Spirit on all flesh." Peter referred to this in his post Pentecost sermon: "These are not drunk as you suppose, since it is only the third hour of the day. But this is that which was spoken by the prophet Joel. (Acts 2:15-16)

It does not take a lot of imagination to know there was a lot of joy on that occasion and whenever there are times of "making melody in your heart to the Lord." As one former and transformed addict told me after a joyous time in the presence of the Lord, he said something to the effect, "Pastor if we could only bottle and sell this, we could cure a lot of addicts—we could call it Jesus' Joy."

I wrote the following in my Challenge Study Bible notes on Ephesians 5:15-20 entitled, BE PEOPLE WITH GOOD SENSE AND NOT LIKE FOOLS: "Paul contrasted those who partied and drank to excess and destroyed themselves with those with good sense. Where do you find such people, and what do you do in contrast to the

41

partygoers? The latter have their own happy hour, not at the bar, but in a Spirit-filled gathering, enjoying a different kind of wine—the new wine of the Spirit of God. You can have a chemically induced high or a Spirit-filled joy. Anyone that has experienced both know the former is a cheap thrill that lasts for moments, and the other lasts for eternity." As I often preach, "The devil's best (if there is such thing) cannot compare with God's least (even if there is such a thing). C.S. Lewis said it better: "Bad cannot succeed even at being bad as truly as good is good."[16]

I realize that in any church service or faith-based, Christ-centered chapel service the presence of the Lord is not always strong and real. But it could be. My friend Jeff Johnson, a Teen Challenge graduate who has often conducted "Spiritual Emphasis" weeks at Adult & Teen Challenges and other similar programs, sends me pictures of altar calls in his services. They are pictures I love: students with hands raised, praying, worshipping and seeking God. Others are kneeling, crying out to God. They are drinking in the Spirit of God. I've seen the changes that take place during such times. Lives are changed. A student on the very urge of leaving gets on his knees and has "a drink from Joel's bar." They stay in the program. They have a reason to do so.

Again, I turn to C.S. Lewis' writings regarding joy and pleasure: "Joy is not a substitute for sex; sex is very often a substitute for joy. I sometimes wonder whether all pleasures are not substitutes for joy."[17]

A convert from years of addiction said, "I was good at being bad. You have to be good as it was defined in that lifestyle to survive and get high. Now that I'm with Jesus, how could I ever want to be bad at this? Now my lows are better than my best highs." As I've pointed out in previous chapters, I have always enjoyed how addicts that have a drink of Jesus' joy describe it in contrast to their old life. The Bible does the same. Song of Solomon 1:2 says, "Thy love is better than wine." That is saying something since, at that time, sweet wine was the beverage of choice.

The title and premise of this book is in the style of the book of the Song of Solomon in which it describes the Jews that Solomon saw as an allegory (moral story) of God's love for Israel, and by Christians as an allegory of Jesus' loving relationship to the church. This helps to understand better the meaning of Song of Solomon 7:9: "Kissing you is more desirous than drinking the finest wine. How wonderful and tasty!" (CEV)

If you are new in Christ, don't feel guilty if you see others who seem to have more joy than you.

The more you know the Lord, the more reasons you too will have to rejoice. Joy, like faith and love, is progressive. Those who ask receive. Those who want more, receive more. "The desire of the righteous is only good" (Proverbs 11:23), especially when that desire is to drink from the cup of the Lord.

One of my favorite authors is A.W. Tozer. He writes, "At the root of all true spiritual growth is a set of right and sanctified desires. The whole Bible teaches that we can have what we want if we want it badly enough. It hardly needs to be said, of course, if our desire is in accordance with the will of God. The desire after God and holiness is the backbone of all real spirituality, and when that desire becomes dominant in life, nothing can prevent us from having what we want. The longing cry of the God-hungry soul can be expressed in the five words of this song, "Oh, to be like Thee." While this longing persists, there will be steady growth in grace and a constant progress towards Christlikeness."[18]

Oh, how I pray drug addicts would be like the four lepers you can read about in the days of Elisha. Four lepers sat outside the gates of Samaria in a time of famine and they knew they were going to die if they did not do something. They said to each other, "Why should we sit here, waiting to die?" (2 Kings 7:3 CEV) They decided if they went inside the city, they might as well starve inside as well as outside the city. That evening, they left for the Syrian camp, not realizing that supernaturally that army heard the sound of chariots and the noise of horses—the noise of a great army—so the Syrians fled, leaving everything behind. Joy awaited the four lepers inside the city where they ate and drank to their hearts' content.

If you're not yet in recovery or just beginning, my question to you is, why stay where you are and die, possibly spiritually and perhaps worse, physically? Supernatural deliverance is available to you just as those lepers experienced. Addiction is a form of leprosy. Get up! Go to a City of Refuge that represents a feast of joy in the Lord. These lepers did something you should do if you found that joy. Tell others. They did, saying to one another, "We are not doing right. This day is a day of good news, and we remain silent. Let us go and tell the King's household." (2 Kings 8:28)

We are the sum total of our desires or to put it another way, what juices you up. Someone reading this needs to hear this: Aren't you tired of drinking at the wrong fountain? Paul wrote, "You cannot drink the cup of demons; you cannot partake of the Lord's Table [communion] and the table of demons." (1 Corinthians 10:21)

It's time to seek the Lord, and if you have found Him and He has found you, don't be a 'more-or-less' Jesus follower—ask for more...more...more!

Chapter 7

JOY ON THE OTHER SIDE OF THE CROSS

"Looking unto Jesus, the author and finisher of our faith, who for the joy set before Him endured the cross, despised the shame, and has sat down at the right hand of the throne of God."

Hebrews 12:2

"No man understands the Scriptures unless he be acquainted with the cross."
—Martin Luther, Table Talk

I fear we preachers are sometimes not forthright with new converts or those who enquire about following Him. We leave out, so to speak, the fine print on the conditions for following our Savior. Of course, there is no "fine print" in the Bible, but what that term stands for is not making clear what it means to commit to serving our Lord—this can be withheld from a new believer.

They will soon find out for themselves and without proper teaching may rethink their commitment. Jesus said, "If anyone desires to come after Me, let him deny himself, and take up his cross daily, and follow Me." (Luke 9:23) This was said right after Peter's declaration to Jesus' question, "Who do you say that I am?" Peter answered and said, "The Christ of God." (Luke 9:20) Then, just before Jesus spoke that, the disciples and all His followers had their own cross to carry. He said, "The Son of Man must suffer many things." He was trying to convey to them what they had a hard time hearing, that the cross meant death for Him in one way and another way for them.

Thus, there are two crosses. One only Jesus could carry the cross as the means of His death; but the other cross that we His followers will face is temptation, trials and testing from following Him. The amazing thing, however, is that Jesus went to His cross, His trial, His rejection, and His death doing it "for the joy set before Him."

James wrote, "Brethren, count it all joy when you fall into various trials." (James 1:2) For me personally, my greatest challenge is to have joy when I am asked to carry my personal cross in following my Savior. I say amen after the trials are over. But

Jesus set the example. He was able to see what came after the cross. I have rarely heard someone give testimony when facing a serious operation, sharing that they were experiencing joy. I have faced board meetings in which I knew I was going to face questions and opposition, but I don't recall feeling joy.

Joy on the other side of the cross is an expected joy, but God's grace is sufficient to experience joy before the cross. One of the believers' greatest challenges, if we are honest, is to "count it all joy" when going through a trial. We can all agree that we learn from our trials; we grow spiritually. But can we, when going into the trial, be joyful before, as well as after?

I don't think counting it all joy means we are oblivious to the seriousness of a trial. That would be denial. If Paul wrote the verse in Hebrews 12:2 (and I believe he did), then he knew something himself about joy before his own cross leading to his death. He wrote an epistle about joy, Philippians, when imprisoned. It's a remarkable writing about joy when Paul had every reason not to be joyful.

Here's a few lessons to be learned about joy before and after carrying his own cross which he describes in Corinthians 11:23-28 as to the following: "imprisonments, beaten nearly to death, bodily lashes, travel dangers, sleepless nights, shipwrecked, homeless, hungry and thirsty and apart from that, there is the daily pressure upon me of concern for all the churches." And you think you got a heavy cross to carry, whatever that may be. As I write primarily to those in recovery and who have had a drink of joy, what are the crosses they can expect to face or are currently facing in which they should count it all joy?

I mention three trials I have witnessed regarding facing fears of those in rehab recovery:

1. **Fear of failure!**

    One student said to me: "Pastor, I have a fear-of-failure mentality. I've failed in almost everything I did and tried in life: jobs, relationships, and I have a record of relapses." I said, "You are not just fearing failure. You fear success." He admitted failure was so ingrained in him that it became like a self-fulfilling prophecy. It's possible to feel more secure in failure than in success. My counsel to him and those like him reading this is to embrace the present. It can seem a cliché, but it's true: "Live one day at a time." Enjoy the present. The verse says Jesus endured the anticipated suffering of the cross because He knew joy followed suffering. But that verse begins with "Looking unto Jesus." Keep your eyes on the prize—Jesus is the prize and He is "the same yesterday, today and forever."

Fear is like binoculars making everything bigger and worse than it is. Turn them around to see what faith does. "Every fear is distrust, and trust is the remedy for fear." (A.B. Simpson)[19]

2. **Fear of the future.**

Two things are tied together; fear of failure either in the now or in the future. The latter has to do with "can I make it to graduation and stay clean after completing the program?" Again, this verse Hebrews 12:2 has a promise, that Jesus is "the author and finisher of our faith." Take one step at a time. Picture the joy of getting your graduation certificate. Anticipate the joy of enduring your testings that are sure to come after you finish the prescribed rehab discipleship program or in whatever way you are seeking recovery.

3. **Fear of family.**

Little is said about this, but one of the tests of endurance for the changed, transformed former addict is rebuilding life after addiction. Family is central to that. Some have burned this bridge so badly there is no biological family to go back to. On the other hand, family estrangement may be temporary. Your parents may be in a wait-and-see period for you to prove yourself. This is a test to anticipate joy on the other side of a cross of broken relationships.

Be patient! Recognize what hurts you may have caused. Hold on to the joy of reunion and fellowship with family. If the situation is irreparable, remember you are now a part of the family of God. Connect with a church family. Build new relationships. Realize however, good relationships usually do not happen overnight. Give yourself and others time to connect with you. Joy is meant to be a shared experience.

There are phases of the Christian life for transformed drug users. One is deliverance and the other is destiny. This is represented in the Israelites crossing the Red Sea (deliverance) and then crossing the Jordan River to claim their inheritance, their Promised Land of destiny. God wants you to land on His promises that He will "never leave you or forsake you." The purpose of deliverance is to then move forward into God's will—His destiny for you.

The children of Israel, when they crossed the Red Sea, sang songs of deliverance with hearts of gratitude for their rescue. David Wilkerson wrote in his Daily Devotional book entitled, *God Is Faithful*:

The children of Israel did offer praise and thanksgiving—but they did it on the wrong side of the Red Sea. The people rejoiced all night after their deliverance, but God took no pleasure in it. Anyone can shout gratitude after the victory comes. The question God put to Israel was, 'Will you praise Me before I send help—while you are still in the midst of the battle?' God help us to sing the right song on the testing side of trials. Are you in a most difficult time? Then sing! Praise! Say to the Lord, 'You can do it—You delivered me before, You can deliver me now. I rest in Your joy.' [20]

◆ ◇

Chapter 8

MY CUP RUNS OVER

◇

*"You serve me a six-course dinner right in front of
my enemies. You revive my drooping head;
my cup brims with blessing."*
Psalm 23:5 MSG

*"One of the greatest gifts we are given is our
emotions. We need not fear our emotions."*
—Rich Hunt [21]

There is a lot of joy expressed in Psalm 23. But
there is also sorrow expressed in reference to
walking through a valley of death. I grew up in a
church where the cup of joy ran over numerous
times. Joy is a feeling—an emotion—and for me,
having a Christianity without having overflowing
cups of joy on occasion, I might as well go to a
football game, instead. I know there is emotion

there with plenty of joy, at least for the winning side. True Christianity is being on the winning side. As such, we should not deny our emotions.

This leads to a question. What do feelings and emotions have to do with spirituality? I find that the emotions of believers found in the Word, the Spirit, and in worship is downplayed too much. Maybe this is the reason many are fleeing from the church, especially young people, in large numbers. Church and chapel services, especially when in attendance by those living in the hopelessness of addiction, ought to be vibrant, challenging, exciting, and inspiring. God's house should be all about life, change, and above all, joy.

A young convert approached me with a question. "Pastor," he said, "for the first few months I was experiencing such joy in the presence of the Lord. But now I've hit a wall. And times, I have flashes of doubt that come in my mind about my salvation. What can you advise me?"

I assured him what he was experiencing was very normal. I said, "As you feed your faith, your doubts and fears will starve to death." Then I said something else that he responded to. I said, "Who would you rather be? A Christian who has flashes of doubt or an atheist or agnostic who has flashes of faith?" He repeated the phrase, "Flashes of faith?" with a questioning look.

He asked, "What do you mean?"

I answered, "You have the Lord and the Word to go to in times of a faith crisis. Pity the unbeliever who has a flash of faith in which he thinks maybe there is a God, maybe all that the Christians say about Jesus is real. Maybe there is a heaven and a hell! Where does he go to deal with such questions of faith when he has lived his whole life having no faith?"

He got excited. "Pastor, I can't wait until I talk to my professor in college tomorrow. I'm going to flash some faith questions to him."

Cups of joy can overflow at times and more often than not, that cup can seem empty or nearly empty.

I once asked a student in rehab, "Are you saved?" He answered, "No, not today." He was serious. It's hard for someone who has depended on a feeling found in a bottle, pill, or powder to then learn how to handle the highs and lows when serving the Lord.

In my counsel with this young man, I reminded him of what he had been taught in a class on How I Can Know I'm Christian. In this class, three important points are listed on receiving salvation: that it is based on Fact, Faith, and Feelings. I went over this with him. The Fact is, "Whoever calls on the name of the Lord shall be saved." (Romans 10:13) Because of Jesus' death on the cross, we receive the gift of salvation. That is a Fact. Faith is accepting this fact on Faith as a continual process. Feelings then follow Fact and Faith.

But here's where the teaching on "Feelings" can be used as a caution to Faith. I could never understand, when I was exposed to church life and traditions outside my Pentecostal upbringing, why many churchgoers as soon as they walk through the door of a church suppress their feelings. If someone raised their hands in worship, or God forbid, says, "Amen" or "Hallelujah" they might be shown the exit door.

I recall when I had contacted the late John Wimber to help me learn how to connect our converts more to local churches. At one point he said, "You have something special here at Teen Challenge because your residents think all Christians worship like they do here in this program. Eventually, they're going to have to learn that not everyone's cup is running over."

I was with a group of pastors at a retreat once. A discussion came up when one pastor asked another pastor (who happened to be Pentecostal), "What do you do about the verse in which Paul writes, 'Let everything be done decently and in order.'?" (1 Corinthians 14:40) It so happens that verse comes at the end of Paul speaking about,

"He who speaks in a tongue" and "he who prophesies." (1 Corinthians 14:2-3) What these pastors also missed is that Paul also said, "Let everything be done..."

I'm not promoting speaking in tongues or a Pentecostal doctrine here, but I do strongly believe that those coming out of addiction need the fullness of the Spirit and to use whatever tongue God gives them to revel in the joy of the Lord on a regular basis. A joy-filled heart and soul finds "the peace that passes understanding." (Philippians 4:7)

Joy does not, should not, depend solely on external things, whether they are pleasant or unpleasant. Joy can co-exist with sorrow and pain. Joy is like salvation in that we can have it always, presently and through eternity.

God is not turned off by shouts of praise. He does not get nervous like some churchgoers who are upset with shouts of halleluiahs. I've seen even so-called charismatic pastors and leaders quench genuine outbursts of joy.

Have you ever been "between a rock and a hard place"? It's not a bad place to be when it's interpreted in the light of Scripture. Moses wrote, "I proclaim the name of the Lord... He is my Rock; His work is perfect." (Deuteronomy 32:3-4) Paul wrote about the Rock (1 Corinthians 10:4) in reference to the Israelites in their wilderness journey saying, "They all ate the same spiritual food, and drank the same spiritual drink. For they drank of the spiritual Rock, that followed them and that Rock was Christ." They, like us today, were between a Rock and a hard place, with the Rock gushing out the Spirit of God, a drink by which we need never to thirst again.

Another C.S. Lewis timely quote from *Surprised by Joy* is spot on (as the English would say, and Lewis was English): "I call joy, which is here a technical term and must be sharply distinguished both from happiness and pleasure. Joy (in my sense) has indeed one characteristic, and one only, in common with them; the fact that anyone who has experienced it will want it again... I doubt whether anyone who has tasted it would ever, if both were in his power, exchange it for all the pleasures in the world." [22]

If your cup of joy has never run over, then run to the Lord, raise your cup up to Him, and ask for a shot of Joy. If your cup used to run over, but now it doesn't, return for a refill. If you want to know about an overabundance of symbolism relative to worship, it is found in the Temple Solomon built. There was a water container for the priests to wash the burnt offing to the Lord and for the priests also to wash in. This was a picture of the cross later given for the forgiveness of sin. So important were these sacrifices and worship and the water associated with it that the Scripture says the containers were "the work of the brim of a cup" (2 Chronicles 4:5 KJV) and it held about 16,500 gallons of water. That's some sized cup! Ephesians 5:26 speaks of the washing of the water of the Word. Our cup of joy is the result of the Word washing us clean of our sins, and that should be a reason to enjoy a cup of joy every day.

Chapter 9

THE DANCE OF JOY

"You did it: you changed wild lament into whirling dance; You ripped off my black mourning band and decked me with wild flowers. I'm about to burst with song; I can't keep quiet enough about you. God, my God, I can't thank you enough."

Psalm 30:11-12 The Message

"Be careful and be warned not to be like the brother of the prodigal who when the lost son returned, he got angry when 'he heard music and dancing,' (Luke 15:24) a celebration of his brother's homecoming."

—Don Wilkerson

Whenever I've seen a couple celebrate their marriage at a reception that followed and they have their first dance—which I've seen mostly on TV, but occasionally at attendance at a wedding—I will say to my wife, Cindy, "I wish we could have danced at our wedding." That was impossible for two reasons: one, we had no reception really, and second if there had been a reception where there was dancing, we could never, ever have danced. The reason: my mother was in attendance and so was my brother's wife, Gwen.

Dancing of any kind was a taboo in our tradition of Christianity, even at a wedding. Even now, when my wife and I see a couple's first dance at a wedding on television, I say to her, "Honey, teach me to dance—with you." She just laughs, even though I'm serious. I know what she's thinking: "You can't teach an old dog new tricks."

The only dancing I have seen outside of a couple after they have said, "I do" is on a rare occasion when it has happened in a church. There is also in some churches "dancing before the Lord" as David did in Old Testament times. But this kind for me will have to wait until I get to heaven, assuming it's allowed there!

"Dance" is mentioned about 30 times in the Bible (King James Version). We can assume that it's always associated with joy. If it is possible to dance in one's heart before the Lord, I have done a lot of that. The closest I have ever come to letting my body move to song, praise, and worship was when I was co-pastor of Times Square Church with my brother David. One of my kids can mimic my very, very low-key bodily response to praise and worship, which is moving their feet a bit and with a right hand lowering it and then slowly raising it heavenward as if leading a choir. So it is said of me, that's what my platform demeanor has been: a bit of dance in my step during times of worship.

Joy does need to be given expression. I have no problem with those in a church service who dance. However, I wonder why, if it's "before the Lord" that they must always come up in front of the church to do it. I also understand those in a church tradition where praise and worship—and joy—is contained in a very conservative manner. I used to criticize those who criticized Pentecostal worship if it was loud, boisterous, and with a few speaking out in another tongue (though nowadays this is rare). I don't criticize the criticizers anymore because I now, on occasion, worship with such believers and I know them to love the Lord and have the joy of the Lord within them.

But still I wonder as Tozer does when he writes, "Have we lost our 'Oh'?" He writes further, "It is a solemn and beautiful thought that in our worship of God there sometimes rushes up from the depths of our souls feelings that all this wealth of words is not sufficient to express. To be articulate at times, we are compelled to fall back on "Oh!" or "O"!

—a primitive exclamatory sound that is hardly a word at all and scarcely admits of a definition."[23]

The best well-known dance in the Bible would be King David doing so upon the return of the Ark of the Covenant back to Jerusalem: "So David and all the house of Israel brought up the ark of the Lord with shouting and with the sound of the trumpet." (2 Samuel 6:16) In the very next verse, we learn that David was "leaping and swirling before the Lord…" (NKJV). The King James Version uses the word "dancing" before the Lord.

The full text of verse 16 reads: "Now as the ark of the Lord came into the City of David, Michal, Saul's daughter, looked through the window and saw King David leaping and whirling before the Lord; and she despised him in her heart." (NKJV) She should have gone herself to meet David and the ark and joined in the celebration. Instead, she was like those who stand afar off when it's time to rejoice in the presence of the Lord. In doing this, I note she is not referred to as David's wife, but Saul's daughter for at that moment, she was more like her father Saul in his pride than David in his humility.

I have seen those who applaud Michal in her "despising David in her heart" as a means of criticizing such that might happen in a church of today or in a modern-day revival. David instead says, "In

God's presence I'll dance all I want! He chose me over your father and the rest of our family and made me prince over God's people, over Israel. Oh yes, I'll dance to God's glory—more recklessly even than this. And as far as I'm concerned...I'll gladly look like a fool...but among these maids you're so worried about, honored no end." (2 Samuel 6:22 MSG) There is another aspect to bringing the ark back to its rightful place. Before this time of dance celebration, David had disobeyed God in the manner which the ark was being brought back to Jerusalem. "And David arose with all the people who were with him...to bring up the ark of God. So they set the ark on a new cart, and brought it..."And it was at this time that "Israel played music before the Lord with all kinds of instruments." (2 Samuel 6:1-5) While the ark was being carried in this manner, a man named Uzzah put his hand on it to steady it and was struck dead. This upset David and he postponed temporarily bringing back the ark to Jerusalem.

I have seen a type of this very thing happening in the ministry my brother and I founded, Adult & Teen Challenge (ATC). In the second oldest such program, it has formed another different organization under a different name in which it does not follow the vision, policies, and the original purpose for which we founded the ministry to take place. Yet it has placed ATC under the non-faith-based entity and in so doing, in my opinion, it is like what happened with the Ark of the Covenant as described above with putting the original ministry on a new cart. We will see how that turns out.

When David responded to Michal's rebuke of her husband dancing, he said to his wife "I was celebrating in honor of Him [the Lord]."

What can we learn from the account of David dancing before the Lord?

1. **Beware of killjoys.**

   If you allow others to do so, they will quench your spirit of joy. I've seen a family (primarily mothers) and on an occasion a spouse unable to deal with the changed life of an addict. Those who have been patient with a loved one's broken life are to be commended. However, a caregiver can turn into a control-giver. I've seen a spouse and even a mother that got so used to being in charge when their loved one was in their before-life that when the loved one returned home, they would not allow him to be the priest in the house. Sad as it may seem that a parent or parents (even a spouse in some cases) would rather be in control of a loved one in such a great need of them and when they get healed they lose their "they need me" role.

I have witnessed a family of Christians serving the Lord in what I termed "moderation" (not a good thing) who wanted the returned son, daughter, or spouse to not be so bold in the Lord. Watch out for the Michals in your home, church, workplace or community if they try to be Joy killers and steal your joy in the Lord.

2. **David, in dancing before the Lord, looked like the average Christian and priest.**

David changed his dress from his kingly robe to what a common priest used when offering praise to the Lord in the Temple. You can overdo your testimony by getting upset if others don't share your enthusiasm for and joy in the Lord. Recognize that you may come off a spiritual high surrounded by others in the lowland of spirituality. Adjust without compromising your relationship to Christ.

In church life, find a David who is able to be the common man relating to common people without downsizing his praise and worship to please the holier-than-thous in the church.

3. **Always identify with those who society may look down on because of their race, culture, or class.**

Michal mocked David because he "uncovered himself...in the eyes of the maidservants [slave girls], as one of the base fellows shamelessly uncovers himself." (2 Samuel 6:21) David was keeping it real. I can imagine the slave girls may have come from a culture where emotion was a virtue and not a shame.

When someone comes out of the hood, the drug culture, or the barroom culture into the faith community, there is the danger of pride and losing contact with the likes of the sinners whom Jesus so often ate with.

Faith expressed with emotion often has to do with personality type, culture, race, and/or church upbringing. My grandfather preacher was quite lively when preaching and worshipping. Someone criticized him, saying that when Solomon's Temple was built the stone blocks were "dressed [prepared] in the quarry so that the building site was reverently quite—no noise from hammers and chisels" was heard. (1 Kings 6:7) Granddad Wilkerson responded, "But you should have been there when they blasted out the rocks." Enough said! "Blessed are the people that know the joyful sound; they shall walk, O Lord, in the light of thy countenance." (Psalm 89:15)

Chapter 10

DRINKING...TOGETHER

*"All the believers met together in one place...
They worshipped together at the Temple each day,
met in homes for the Lord's Supper,
and shared their meals with great joy
and generosity."*

Acts 2:44-46 NLT

*"He [God] never intended that salvation
should be received by the individual apart
from the larger company of believers."*

—A.W. Tozer [24]

One thing a barroom can have that sometimes is lacking in the church: camaraderie (mutual trust and friendship among those who spend a lot of time together). A gathering of believers in church, small groups like Celebrate Recovery, and other similar groups are necessary for recovery healing. Those who do not find it (or seek it) have higher incidents of relapse.

I used to watch a TV sitcom called "Cheers" (until it got too raunchy). What caught my attention every time it came on was a by-line that said, "Cheers—where everybody knows your name." I'd always think to myself, "That's what the church is or should be—a place where everybody knows your name." I have always had both a positive and negative response to A.A. (Alcoholics Anonymous). It is a place of acceptance, honesty, and confession. However, it prevents those who attend from being part of a healing community where they can be among those who are spiritually whole in Christ.

When speaking once in Florida and praying for those who came forward to dedicate or rededicate themselves to the Lord, I asked one young man probably in his late 20's, "What can I pray for, for you?" He said, "I have accepted the Lord, but something's missing." I found out the only friends he had known were at a bar he frequented. Then I knew what was missing. He needed to be with new faces, believers and not barroom drinkers. I took him over to a group of young people in the first row and asked them to invite him out for food, fellowship, and exchange stories of drinking in the

New Wine of the Spirit. Even the non-believers on the Day of Pentecost mocking the believers, said, "They are full of new wine." (Acts 2:13)

We speak of those who come to Christ for salvation as having a "personal experience" with Him. That it is, and should be. Each must be born-again individually by the Spirit of God. But once born of the Spirit, the faith walk is not for Lone Rangers; but as the Psalmist wrote, "How wonderful and pleasant when brothers [and sisters] live together in harmony." (Psalm 133:1 NLT)

Why should the world's drinkers be the only ones to have fellowship based on an adult beverage that brings them together? It is a false "Happy Hour" often based on similar miseries, trying to escape real relationships. "I'll drink to that." I ask what is "that"?

If you are in a recovery program, make sure when you complete it that you find a "good and pleasant" environment to be a part of. If you are on your own personal faith journey of recovery sponsored by a church, become a part of that church or a similar one.

One of the songs sung when God's people journeyed to the Jerusalem Temple, called "A Song of Ascent," is from Psalm 126. I quote verse 1-3. Note the words I italicize:

When the LORD brought back the captivity of Zion, *we* were like those that dream. Then *our* mouth was with laughter, and *our* tongue with singing. Then they said among the nations, 'The LORD had done great things for *them*.' The LORD has done great things for *us*, and *we* are glad.

Note the words "our, they, them, us and we."

Too many complain about the imperfections of the church and when they do so, they are complaining about themselves because the "church" is more than an organization body of people. It is everyone born of God. Like it or not, we are all members of the mystical body called the church— the Family of God for better or worse. Make it better by your attendance and involvement.

Charles Spurgeon wrote, "The day we find the perfect church, it becomes imperfect the moment you join it."[25] Join it! You will find it a place with people just like yourself and God loves them all. Loners in the faith deprive themselves of the healing possibilities of being in the Household of Faith. "Forsake not the assembling of ourselves together" (Hebrews 10:25) is especially for those who may have come from a dysfunctional family or one they helped to fracture. There are brothers and sisters waiting for the recovery and recovered ones to be introduced to them. They are full of faith, love, and joy and just waiting to share a drink with others of the new wine of the Spirit. True friends stick by us. They walk a thin line between total acceptance of us and holding us accountable. They should keep confidences, but not at the cost of condoning sin.

A further quote from the same book of A.W. Tozer quoted above is, "The Christian who withdraws from the fellowship of other Christians will suffer great soul injury. Such a one can never hope to develop normally. He'll get too much of himself and not enough of other people; and that is not good."[26]

If you are in a faith-based recovery program, residential or otherwise, here's what you should have learned; or yet need to learn.

1. **Share your joy! Drink together with another or others.**

    "And let us consider how we may spur one another on towards love and good deeds, not giving up meeting together, as some are in the habit of doing, but encourage one another..." (Hebrews 10:24-25 NIV) Don't think when joining a group you have to give up your individuality. Instead, celebrate it and in doing so, enjoy what others can do to help keep you from blind spots in your life. We need the Jesus in each other to know more of Jesus.

2. **Listen to others. Drink from their cup of Joy.**

"Love each other as brothers and sisters. Be tender hearted, and keep a humble attitude." (I Peter 3:8 NLT)

"No one is wise enough to live alone, nor good enough nor strong enough. God has made us to a large degree dependent upon each other. From our brethren we can learn how to do things, and sometimes also we can learn how not to do them." (Tozer) [27]

Paul writes: "Let the peace of Christ keep you in tune with each other. None of this going off and doing your own thing. Cultivate thanksgiving." (Colossians 3:15-16 MSG) I have always loved the graduation celebrations when students finish the program and are given a Certificate of Completion. It's not unusual during testimony time for a student to publicly thank another student or students for in part helping reach their night of accomplishment. A friend—the right kind of one—can be someone to drink joy together with and encourage you in your walk with God.

3. **Respect your Joy-Tender.**

If the Apostle Paul can make a contrast and warning between those who are excessive in their drinking and that of being filled with the Spirit, I hope no one is offended by my comparing a bartender with a Pastor. I call the former one who serves up drinks in a barroom and the latter serving up drinks in and of the Spirit in a church.

To become a bartender, it takes about four hours of training plus completing a written examination. A pastor on the other hand can take as much as four years to train for the ministry in order to serve a congregation where he offers the water of Life and the New Wine of the Spirit to thirsty souls. Every new believer needs a man of God to serve drinks of joy including a good solid spiritual meal. Addiction is often done in isolation; recovery requires being connected to new friends and the family of God. Sheep need a flock and the flock need a shepherd. Next to God, we need friendship, fellowship, and a shepherd to help guard, guide, and graze us. Remember that shepherds, the good and right ones, always stay with the sheep.

Chapter 11

ME AND LARNELLE HARRIS: I CHOOSE JOY

"I know that nothing is better for them than to rejoice, and to do good in their life."

Ecclesiastes 3:12

"Satan offers you what he cannot give; he is a liar, and has been from the foundation of the world."[28]

—D.L. Moody

You may have never heard of Larnelle Harris. He's a gospel singer and songwriter. I met him twice. I'm sure he would not remember me. It was many years ago. We were together at two different banquets; he was the guest soloist and I was the speaker. At the time, he was still an up-and-coming musician and the thing that stands out most in my memory is that his traveling assistant told me, "Larnelle really enjoyed your messages." My sole reason for bringing up about me and Larnelle is that sometime later he wrote a song I well remember and the song in some ways is part of my testimony. The title is, "I Choose Joy." I did not even know he wrote the song until I googled the lyrics to find out who wrote it. A few lines of it are:

> I choose joy.
> I'll never let the problems keep me down
> 'Cause I know the Lord will work things out
> For my good. I choose joy, joy.[29]

Joy is not determined like happiness is. Happiness is determined by the good and enjoyable things, circumstances, and the unexpected "happenings" in our lives. Joy results also from those things, but joy is much deeper. Joy comes from within, not entirely from outside us. Joy kicks in, or can and should when we do as Larnelle writes above: "I'll never let the problems get me down." In the world of drugs you can take "uppers and downers," things to stimulate and things to sedate you. Is that the way you want to live? Living on "upper" days and "downer" days?

Joy is like a steady stream coming up from within you.

Charles Swindoll wrote, "Joy is a choice. It's a matter of attitude that stems from one's confidence in God that He is at work, that He is in the midst of whatever has happened, is happening, and will happen. Either we fix our minds on that and determine to laugh again, or we will wail and whine our way through life. We determine which way we will go."[30]

Because joy is a blessing from God within us, it is always there. We just need to give expression to it. "Let everything that has breath praise the Lord." (Psalm 150:6) Praise will lift you high above feelings of hurt, anger, injustice, loneliness and sadness over the troubles we and others may experience. This does not mean trying to manufacture joy. Either Christ dwells within us and we recognize it or He does not. My father, a pastor, used to talk about church member's responses when asked how they were doing. They'd say, "Pastor, under the circumstances we're okay." My father responded, "You don't need to be under your circumstances, but above them."

This is why having joy is a command. God commands it because He gives it to us as a fruit of the Spirit. When you have it, enjoy it. Joy is more beautiful than sorrow and sadness. Once you make this all-important discovery, embrace it as a moral obligation. Joy is for when we go through the storm, as well as when it's over.

I've watched addicts relapse. It does not happen the moment they inject themselves, drink, or pop pills—it happens long before that. It is when they put a cap on their heart and soul and fail to walk in the fullness of the Spirit. They quit praying. The Word is no longer sweet to their taste (Psalm 109: 103). During praise and worship, they are spectators instead of participants.

Drug addicts know what a "connection" means. I spoke to a young man in our rehab program and he complained he didn't have faith. I said, "Yet you had enough faith to connect with your drug supplier. You made the exchange, never knowing if you got good stuff or bad, or if it could even kill you. Why treat God with less faith than in your 'connection'?" Yes, this is why I write about a drug called joy. But you have to connect with the supplier—connect with a heavenly connection.

One of the great stories in the Bible is about when Jesus sat at Jacob's Well and a woman came to draw water. A Samaritan woman arrived to draw from the well. We might say she was addicted to men. She had been married and divorced five times and the man she was living with when she met Jesus was not her legal husband.

She came to draw water at the noon hour. In that time and culture respectable women drew water early in the day, not in the heat of the noon-day sun. But she had a reputation. She must have felt unwelcomed by other respectable women. So she brings her water pot to draw water from the well. Her water pot was as empty as her soul and her life.

Jesus then gave her living water. (John 4:25-26) What did she then do? She did two things: "The woman left her water pot." Why? Jesus gave her water by which she would never thirst again. Second, "She went her way into the city, and said to the men..." (John 4:29) She was a woman attracted to men, but now she must have gone to the very men she once was attracted to in a certain way, but now going to them in a different way as a different person. It's not too hard to imagine the joy she experienced in encountering Jesus and then sharing the news about Him.

> So, when I find myself under a load
> Of circumstances and care
> God wants to know
> What I'm doing under there.
> Well, I know what to choose, joy.
> I choose joy.

This woman not only carried a water pot to Jacob's Well, but she also carried guilt, shame, and an unsatisfied religion. What choices did this woman have before she met Jesus? We don't know, but it's doubtful she had the ability to choose joy. You do—if Jesus lives inside you. You can let life's problems and challenges quench the Spirit of joy implanted in you. You can wallow in self-pity, self-condemnation, moping around having a pity-party. The problem with a "pity-party" is that you are the only one in attendance, and in such a state of mind you are not good company alone with such feelings.

I chose Joy. I hope you have, or will, also. Does Jesus live within you? Regardless of what you may be going through: fear of the future, fear of relapse, fear of more failure in your life, fear of many unknowns, you too can choose joy.

One ship sails east
One sails west
Regardless of how the winds blow.
Tis the set of the sail
and not the gale
that determines the way we go.

—Ella Wheller Wilcox

Choosing joy will help you do three things:

1. **Choose joy over the pleasures of the world.**

Pleasure is not all bad unless they take the place of our joy in the Lord. If they do, they may as well be treated as evil. However, there is joy in natural things that can have a spiritual effect on us. One of my favorite movies is Chariots of Fire. The line I love is Eric Liddell the Olympic runner being asked why he ran. He answered, "Because I feel His pleasure" when he ran.

Choose life's joy, both the natural ones and the ones that are distinctly spiritual. If you are new in running this race, do so in a manner that you feel God's pleasure and joy in all things in your life that align with His will for you.

2. **Chose joy over rejection.**

There will always be joy-killers. One type of robber of your joy is well-meaning Christians who see all of life as half-empty. They find many reasons for gloom, but few reasons for joy. Love them, but keep your distance or they will want to serve you their cup of sadness.

Usually those who have been forgiven much love much. Jesus said those forgiven of many sins often show more love than the goody-two-shoe type of person. (Luke 7:44-48) If you have been delivered from an addiction—drugs, alcohol, sex, gambling or whatever—don't let anyone tell you when you talk about your past that you're glorifying the devil. That can happen, but like the Prodigal Son, raise your drink of joy in thanksgiving for your new life until joy spills out all over the place.

3. **Choose joy amid sorrow.**

When we have joy, there can be times of sorrow—sorrow over losses of various kinds. Sorrow can happen side by side with joy, but in turn, joy can run side by side with sorrow. The joy of salvation need never leave us regardless of what happens to us on the outside. Our salvation is eternal, but sorrow need not be eternal. It diminishes over time, but joy need not. All sorrows, suffering, and pains in life will surrender to joy. Let joy be the engine and sorrow the caboose.

4. **Choose joy—the devil cannot compete with it.**

In the waning hours of King David's life, the wrong man was vying for the throne. His name was Adonijah. He thought he had the upper hand to succeed David. He, the Scriptures say, "exalted himself: and he had an entourage of chariots and horsemen, and fifty men to run before him." (1 Kings 1:5) All the trappings of a king awaiting coronation. Just before his demise, this happened: There was a sound Adonijah heard in the City of David (that never was going to be the City of Adonijah), that sound was the celebration of Solomon being anointed King. (Read 1 Kings, Chapter One) Adonijah was eating a meal when Jonathan the son of a priest arrived. He assumed this meant good news, but was told that King David had made Solomon king. The Scriptures also say of this turn of events, "Moreover the kings 'servants have come to bless our lord King David saying, 'May God make the name of Solomon better than your name, and may He make his throne greater than your throne.'" (1 Kings 1:47)

And so it was. Adonijah ended up falling down before Solomon. This is an example that when we are doing God's will, chosen of God to serve His purposes, the devil will not play dead. But one thing is sure. He cannot provide what God can for His chosen. And one of those things is joy; after all, it is the joy of the Lord and not the joy of Satan. All he has to offer is counterfeits and fake replacements for joy. Even the word cannot be used in reference to Satan. Joy draws a circle around you where Satan cannot enter.

Choose joy and as you enjoy the joy of the Lord, all Satan can do is offer you what you have already experienced of his substitutes for joy. Joy is supernatural and the devil can only deal in the natural and make it look super, when in reality it is stupid if you really examine it honestly.

Allow me to put this in terms of a football game. Let's say a team gets the ball on their own one-yard line and they move towards the opponent's goal posts: yard by yard, first down by first down, sometimes by running the ball, at other times passing it. The defense cannot stop them. The offense has the ball and whoever has the ball and keeps moving it, controls the game. All the other side can do is watch the offense moving unstoppable.

The football is joy. The devil can't compete with joy. He tried and for a time, succeeded in your life. But now the ball is in your hands. Never give it up because as long as you have a ball called "joy" the devil can do nothing to stop your progress towards the goal. Keep him on the sidelines until, in the end, he will go to the Lake of Fire. Why go there with him? Live each day in the joy of the Lord because the devil can't compete with what the Lord supplies.

Chapter 12

ISAAC: "HELLO, MY NAME IS LAUGHTER!"

*"So she [Sarah] laughed and said to herself,
"Now that I am worn out and my husband is old,
will I really know happiness?"*

Genesis 12:12 CEV

"Laughter is the closest thing to the grace of God."
—Karl Barth, Theologian

(Author's note: Lest anyone think I have not made a strong enough case for biblical joy and laughter, I finish with this chapter.)

Imagine when Abraham and Sarah's miracle birth child turned thirteen and he was asked his name and he said, "My name is laughter." In God giving his parents the name Isaac before he was born—a name that means laughter—he would have had the last laugh. What kind of a God gives a child the name "laughter"? Because it was, and is, a holy laughter.

The Scriptures mention two kinds of laughter attributed to God. One is a scornful laugh such as quoted in Psalm 2:4: "But the one who rules in heavens laughs; the Lord scoffs at them." The second one is a joyful laughter following deliverance, such as Psalm 126:1-2. "When the Lord brought back His exiles…it was like a dream! We were filled with laughter, and we sang for joy." (NLT)

Why name a son named, "He laughs"? According to the NIV Study Bible, it reads in answer to the question I pose: "Perhaps [giving his parents a name that means laughter] it is revealing some of God's humor. Some think it was to remind Abraham and Sarah how they laughed in disbelief when they heard God's promise [that they would have a son]. But [the name Isaac] seems less like a rebuke than a play on words that proclaim the power of God. It turned their laughter of disbelief into the joyous laughter of a promise fulfilled.

During the course of our working together, my brother David said many encouraging and kind words to me. When I resigned from Times Square Church after helping him co-found it, I told him I was going to leave to start Global Teen Challenge which would help launch the first ministry we founded together in various overseas locations. David said to me, "Don, you can't leave. You understand grace." He, of course, did as well, but I had more opportunities to be a pastor of grace, having worked and helped and given hope to so many addicts.

If *A Drink Called Joy* was going to be made like a natural drink, it would have a mixture of grace, mercy, and truth. John 1:14 says that Jesus came from the Father, "full of grace and truth." Grace without truth is too often cheap grace, and truth without grace can wound rather than heal.

I was born into a home where truth was like a laser beam and grace like a flashlight. In my first year of Bible training in a three-year Bible Institute, I encountered some good biblical training. However, it had an atmosphere where we were treated like children who had to be held in check by what I considered silly rules. The campus life there was very rule-based. We students were on a demerit system whereby if you broke a rule, a demerit went on your record and we were only allowed so many rule infractions per semester. Prior to our Christmas break, I left the school without permission to go home to work as an extra postal deliverer to earn some much-needed funds. I received a large sum of demerits for that, added to my existing number. I ended up with enough demerits to last four years—at a three-year school. Nevertheless, I was determined to have some fun in spite of an unwritten rule that if you were going to be a minister, it was forbidden to laugh or have fun in the process. I learned that theology and laughter were not to mix, but I never learned it very well.

Then I discovered the writings of A.W. Tozer. He wrote on holiness without being holier-than-thou. He wrote prophetically of carnality in the church, yet he never sought financial profit or popularity from his writings. Tozer did not write to be accepted, but to be a watchman. In his book of short essays entitled, *The Root of the Righteous*, one of the chapters caught my eye. It's entitled, *God is Easy to Live With*. His words jumped up off the page:

> The fellowship of God is delightful beyond all telling. He communes with His redeemed ones in an easy and uninhibited fellowship that is restful and healing to the soul... He is quick to mark simple efforts to please Him, and just as quick to overlook imperfections when He knows we meant to do His will.[31]

Tozer went on to speak of those who serve God "grimly... doing right without enthusiasm and joy." He added, "How good it would be that we learn that God is easy to live with."

I grant that there is not much written about humor and laughter in the Christian life, but as theologian Karl Barth taught, since grace is a twin to laughter and because there is a kind of joyous laughter, this belongs in a book about the answer to addiction. Anyone who has lived on artificial feelings, walking around as if on life-support found in a powder, pill, drink, or weed desperately needs *A Drink Called Joy*.

For Abraham, having a son called Laughter did not mean life was always about being happy and joyful. Not when the Lord told him to sacrifice his son as an offering to God as if he was equivalent to the animal sacrifice God was going to later institute in the time of Moses. How ironic that God was asking Abraham to lay his son Laughter on the altar and put a knife in him. Solomon wrote there is "a time to weep and a time to laugh." (Ecclesiastes 3:4 NIV) On Mount Moriah, it was a serious time of testing for Abraham.

Joy does not mean there are not times of sorrow, suffering, and necessary sacrifice in following our Lord. There are two important truths we can learn from Abraham's test:

1. **Like Abraham, we are called to lay our Isaacs on the altar.**

   If you have not heard the expression of "laying your Isaac on the altar" you need to know what it is. We all have an "Isaac" that we dearly love. This is not necessarily something of the world we have to give up. It can be something that is very good that the Lord wants us to die to it, to sacrifice on God's altar.

My sister Ruth gave up a college grant to work with my dad in our church as we moved across the state to another pastoral assignment. When I got a Dear John letter of rejection from the girl I thought would be my wife, I felt God was asking me to accept it. (I didn't think He wanted me to be celibate. At least I hoped not!) It was not the case, and we eventually got married. But Cindy became my "Isaac" that I had to lay on the altar, for a time.

If you're in rehab-recovery and you have your future all planned out in your mind, are you willing to lay that Isaac on the altar?

What is your Isaac?

2. **The story of the willing sacrifice on Mount Moriah ends joyously because of "a ram in a bush." (Genesis 22:11)**

The end of Abraham's test is that "obedience is better than sacrifice." (1 Samuel 15:22) The wonderful thing about giving up an Isaac on the altar is that it's just a version of what I call a "rest stop" (test stop) on the way to God supernaturally providing for you "a ram in the bush." As Abraham took the knife to slay his son, an angel told him to stop—that is the test stop. All of us may face times when we are asked to lay our Isaac on the altar. And what follows?

THREE ISAACS YOU MAY NEED TO LAY ON THE ALTAR!

1. **Time!**

Being a disciple of Christ takes time. If you short-cut it, you will have less chance of staying clean from your addiction and staying pure from the world. It is the "pure in heart" who will see God. (Matthew 5:8) If you are planning to leave before it's God's time, surrender your time to God. Both on earth and in heaven when you are in Christ "time shall be no more." In other words, you will not live your life by your own time schedule, but God's. You can either do time God's way or your way—the latter might do you in, and you may have to then serve time in your old prison.

2. **Impatience!**

A lady came the bookstore counter, banged upon it with her fist, and yelled out, "I want a book on patience, and I want it now!" The impatience I speak of here (besides not being willing to "do time" as God wants you to do it) is the impatience with people, places, and provision. You're with people that may rub you the wrong way, but so what —anywhere and everywhere people will either be a problem or a solution to you. It's your decision. The place where you are at probably has a lot to be desired, but it's where God has put you, so stay put in place. Do you really want to go back to the places that are not fit for humans?

Your provision may now not be as adequate to your liking, but it's probably a lot better than the alternative. Do you want to eat and drink off the devil's table or enjoy the provisions you do have? Do your time in the place where you are and someday God will blow your mind with provisions.

3. **Slothfulness!**

The word you may be more familiar with is laziness. There are three types of slothfulness:

a) Physical. If you're in a program, place, or home being run right they will not let you be lazy. That means you're in a good program.

b) Mental laziness is letting your mind drift into no man's land—that's the place where you give up dreams, holy desires, and goals.

c) Spiritual laziness includes all that's written above plus spiritually you become self-satisfied and coast through the day— even though you can put on a good act and others think you're doing good or okay. But if you stop growing after some weeks or months, then spiritually you are not where you could be. Don't coast! Put your spiritual gears in drive and move forward or before you know it, you will be either in neutral, park, or reverse spiritually. God told Moses, "Speak unto the children of Israel...to go forward." (Exodus 14:15)

Consider what happened to Abraham when be obeyed the Lord in respect to people, places, and provision: (1) "I will make of thee a great nation, I will bless thee, and make thy name great; and thou shalt be blessed." (Genesis 12:2 KJV) (2) "Unto thy seed will I gave this land." (3) "And Abram was very rich in cattle, in silver, and in gold." (Genesis 13:2)

Abram laughed all the way to the bank—of heaven. So will you if you drink from the cup called Joy!

A WORD TO THOSE NEEDING RECOVERY

Don't settle for a short-term treatment program. It took you a long time to become addicted. Don't settle for a shortcut to freedom. Find a true faith-based Christ-centered program. Beware: there are those who call themselves faith based but they trade off the name just to get clients. A place that calls residents "clients" is probably not faith based.

When applying, ask if the residents are called "students" and ask if they have a discipleship long-term program. If you want a long-term cure, find a long-term program.

If you need a referral, write to me at beholdm416@gmail.com

IF YOU ARE CURRENTLY IN RECOVERY

Stay strong and stay in place. Paul writes in 1 Corinthians 9:26-27 in The Message: "I don't know about you, but I'm running hard for the finish line. I'm giving it everything I've got. No lazy living for me. I'm staying alert and in top condition."

Make that your testimony. Read the above at least once a week. Only the weak never finish. To-day and every day is "the rest of your life" One day at a time is all you have to do, repeated until your finish. What joy awaits you upon graduation.

FOR FAMILY AND FRIENDS OF
SOMEONE NEEDING RECOVERY OR
IN RECOVERY

Would you go to a doctor who never cures anyone? To a mechanic who knows nothing about how to repair an engine? Or eat at a restaurant that serves bad food?

The most important decision one will ever make is when referring a family member or friend for help. The next most important decision is where to refer him or her. There are many options today for addiction treatment because it is a big money-making business that subscribes to the disease model of addiction. This disease model says addiction is incurable, thus guaranteeing them clients of those who go in and out of a short-term treatment program like a car goes through a car wash and comes out clean; but only until it gets dirty again. The drug treatment business is a dirty business.

Don't waste your time or the addict's time looking for the wrong treatment. A God-centered, Christ-centered place is the best place and best hope for a permanent cure to addiction. There are thousands that are living proof of this.

Please pass this book and this Afterword message on to others.

OTHER RESOURCES AND
BOOKS RECOMMENDED

A 28-minute documentary produced for Brooklyn Teen Challenge on YouTube entitled, *The Remedy: No Other Cure.*

BOOK TITLE HELPS FOR ADDICTS AND
THOSE WHO WANT TO HELP THEM
By Don Wilkerson

1. *The First Step to Freedom* (write to this email beholdm416@gmail.com for ordering information.)

2. *The Impact of Ordinary People: 30 Lessons from Lessor-Known Men of the Bible* (Book 1) Order at Amazon.com

3. *The Impact of Ordinary People: Lesser-Known Women of the Bible* (Book 2) - Amazon

4. *The Jeremiah Code* - Amazon

5. *Kept From Falling* - Amazon

6. *The Challenge Study Bible* - Amazon

7. *Hope Needs an Address* (Julie Klose, author) - Amazon

8. *The Girl in the Red Dress* - Amazon

9. *Keeping the Cross Central* - Amazon

PROJECT HOPE

The following is a description of one of the faith-based discipleship rehab programs I recommend. I include it for those who may not know what such a program and ministry is. The information below is about Project Hope.

LENGTH OF PROGRAM:

Our program is one year long. Not 30 days, not 90 days, not 11 months. [We are] a year long program [commitment]. There is ample science to back up the need for long term treatment; your brain takes about 14 months on average to start functioning normally again. Plus, I have never run into someone looking for a program [when they were in addiction] giving less than a year commitment [to it], so you can give the same [commitment] to recovery.

NICOTINE SMOKING POLICY:

We don't allow nicotine of any kind. I know that today there are many Christian programs that are compromising in this area, but that's what it is; it's compromise. Even the secular recovery programs can show you the data that those who don't give up nicotine along with their drug of choice are as much as 1% more likely to relapse FOR EVERY CIGARETTE SMOKED per day in sobriety.

COST OF PROGRAM:

We are a free program; we are not an easy program. Everyone is expected to put their hand to the plow and follow a tight daily schedule. Addiction breeds chaos, and we strive to instill discipline and a solid work ethic. We have work in the wood shop, fundraising, marketing, event staffing, flea-markets, as well as working in the community and partnering with churches.

THE JESUS DISCIPLESHIP PART OF THE PROGRAM:

We believe what the Bible says. You'll get a steady dose of the Word through church services, weekday chapels, attending events, along with daily devotion and Scripture memorization. You don't have to be a hardcore Christian to come into the program, and honestly, it's sometimes those individuals that have the toughest time anyway. You don't have to know a single Scripture, but we're going to introduce you to Jesus and hopefully be the place where you can develop a personal relationship with Him.

DAILY PROGRAM LIFE:

We will love you [the residents] and not enable bad behavior or destructive decisions. Sometimes love has to come in the form of telling you a hard truth, or bringing correction in an area of your life. We don't expect perfection out of anyone, just a willingness to remain teachable and learn a new way to live life. I'd rather you be alive and think that I'm too blunt. There's nothing I hate more than seeing someone lost in addiction lose their life to it.

COMPLETION OF PROGRAM:

We will help you after completing your program. We offer paid internships to anyone that graduates our program, as well as opportunities for staff positions after 6 months. Additionally, we have staff housing available, and will continue to support any graduate that needs housing and is pursuing employment outside of the ministry. We're not giving anyone a certificate of completion and kicking them to the curb or forcing them back into a toxic environment.

STAFFING:

We've been there. 90% of our staff members have been through one of our programs, or a similar program. We know the struggle, and we know the solution. Anyone that is a staff member here is here because they want someone else to experience the same freedom that they have now found. There's nothing more rewarding.

We have men's and women's programs in TX, FL, AR, MS & TN.

With thanks to:

Michael Vecchio

COO Of Project Hope & Saving Grace

2013 Graduate of New York Adult &
Teen Challenge

projecthoperc.com

savinggracewh.com

ENDNOTES

1 Lewis, C.S. *The Great Divorce* (Collected Letters of C.S. Lewis). HarperCollins. Kindle Edition.

2 Lewis, C.S. *Surprised by Joy*. HarperCollins. Kindle Edition.

3 Lewis, C.S. *The Great Divorce* (Collected Letters of C.S. Lewis).

4 Ironside, H.A. *Expository Addresses on the Epistle to the Ephesians (Ironside Commentary Series Book 35)*. CrossReach Publications. Kindle Edition.

5 Lewis, C.S. *Letters to Malcolm: Chiefly on Prayer* (San Diego: Harvest, 1964), 92-93.

6 Lewis, C.S. *Surprised by Joy*. HarperCollins. Kindle Edition.

7 St. John of the Cross. *The Collected Works of St. John of the Cross* [Revised Edition]. ICS Publications. Kindle Edition.

8 Tozer, A.W. *The Root of the Righteous* (Sea Harp Timeless series). Sea Harp Press. Kindle Edition.

9 Swindoll, Charles R. *Laugh Again*. Thomas Nelson. Kindle Edition.

10 Lewis, C.S. *The Case For Christianity* (New York: Touchstone Books) 1996.

11 Cummings, Edward Estlin. *Poetry by E.E. Cummings*. Read Books Ltd. Kindle Edition.

12 Barth, Karl. *The Harper Book of Quotations*. Harper Collins. Kindle Edition.

13 Tillich, Paul. *The Courage to Be. Second Edition*. (New Haven, Yale University) 2000 (1st ed. 1952).

14 Edwards, Jonathan. *The Works of Jonathan Edwards: Volume I & II*. Kindle Edition.

15 Lewis, C.S. *Reflections on the Psalms*. HarperCollins. Kindle Edition.

16 Lewis, C.S. *The Great Divorce* (Collected Letters of C.S. Lewis). HarperCollins. Kindle Edition.

17 Lewis, C.S. *Surprised by Joy.* HarperCollins. Kindle Edition.

18 Tozer, A.W. *The Root of the Righteous* (Sea Harp Timeless Series). Sea Harp Press. Kindle Edition.

19 Simpson, Albert Benjamin. *Days of Heaven Upon Earth.* Kindle Edition.

20 Wilkerson, David. *God Is Faithful: A Daily Invitation into the Father Heart of God* (p. 320). Baker Publishing Group. Kindle Edition.

21 Hurst, Rich. *Courage to Connect: A Journey Towards Intimacy in Relationships.* (Colorado Springs: Chariot Victor Publishing, 2002)

22 Lewis, C.S. *Surprised by Joy*. HarperCollins. Kindle Edition.

23 Tozer, A.W. *The Root of the Righteous* (Sea Harp Timeless Series). Sea Harp Press. Kindle Edition.

24 Tozer, A.W. *Born After Midnight* (Camp Hills: Wing Spread) 1989.

25 Spurgeon Charles, *The Best Donation, an Exposition of 2 Corinthians 8:5* delivered on April 5, 1891 at the Metropolitan Tabernacle in London, England.

26 Tozer, A.W. *Born After Midnight* (Camp Hills: Wing Spread) 1989.

27 Ibid.

28 Moody, Dwight Lyman, *Addresses*, Google Books.

29 Harris, Larnelle. *I Choose Joy.* (1992)

30 Swindoll, Charles R. *Laugh Again.* Thomas Nelson. Kindle Edition.

31 Tozer, A.W. *The Root of the Righteous* (Sea Harp Timeless Series). Sea Harp Press. Kindle Edition.